design series Encounters: Lili Fleury
layout: Eleinad Ereivir & Thierry Fontaine (photos)
cover: Thierry Fontaine -*L'Ile habitée*, 2002

SERIES ENCOUNTERS

DIRECTED BY DANIÈLE RIVIÈRE

School Spirit

Pierre Huyghe & Douglas Coupland

Spread Wide

Kathy Acker, Paul Buck, John Cussans, Rebecca Stephens

Life Extrême-an Illustrated Guide to New Life

Eduardo Kac & Avital Ronell

You know where I'm at and I know where you're at

Gary Hill & Martin Cothren

HAVE YOU EVER SEEN A NOMAD IN A HURRY?

GILLES CLÉMENT & THIERRY FONTAINE

TRANSLATED BY
PAUL BUCK & CATHERINE PETIT

ENCOUNTERS

SUMMARY

DON'T BELIEVE THAT FREEING ONESELF IS TO BE ONESELF, IT IS TO INVENT ONESELF AS ANOTHER SELF.

ALAIN DSAMASIO

CONSIDERED
FROM A ZOOLOGICAL
POINT OF VIEW,
IN THE ANATOMIC
PROPERTIES OF HIS BODY,
MAN RISKS REMAINING UNNOTICED, UNRECOGNISED,
DROWNED AMIDST
BEINGS THAT
SURROUND HIM.

JEAN PIVETEAU

FAITH REVEALS TO US THAT GOD
CREATED MAN OUT OF MUD
AND OUR EYES SHOW US
HE REMAINS THAT WAY.

R.P. STOCKIUS

Who's who? Asks the guide, talking to the tourists on holiday. We don't know and it doesn't matter. Bodies appear and disappear in the daylight without saying their name; by depriving themselves of an identity, they defy the law.

* * *

One thing is certain: they don't have a number.
Their freedom is acted upon blindly. With hands, with feet, with fists. With the body offered to the raw matter and who cares about the roughness of the ground or its coolness, it's enough to say it all without opening one's mouth.
Then one listens.

THE BODY NEEDS TO FORGET ITSELF IN ORDER TO THINK.

PASCAL QUIGNARD

THE CHARM OF *JE-NE-SAIS-QUOI* ACTIVATED

VLADIMIR JANKÉLÉVITCH

REALITY HAS MORE IMAGINATION THAN US.

EDGAR MORIN

...THEY ONLY COME IN AN INVISIBLE WAY.

AND THEY RESIDE IN MASKS ON DAYS OF DANCING

AND CELEBRATION IN A MYSTICAL WAY.

OCTAVE. MANNONI

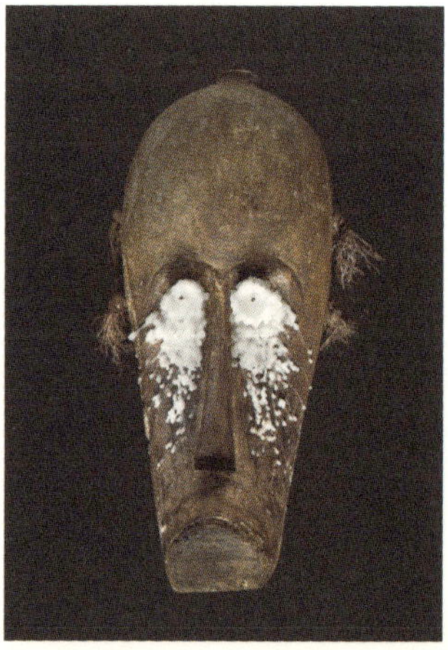

IN LOVE
AS IN BEAUTY
EVERY TRUE LOOK
IS AN EXCHANGED LOOK.

FRANÇOIS CHENG

If the flame is in the eyes, nothing gets extinguished. The look is imprinted in memory, it still burns. Sometimes it sheds tears but it never shies away, it fixes the precise time when everything has been said. It insists on the message by letting the wrinkles, the folds, the possible smiles of the face speak. It maintains the speech in suspense.

* * *

No one can stop the logorrhoea of silence, one stares and it's enough to write a story. Evidently wooden masks have a tongue of glass, it's transparent and doesn't stop thrashing about.

* * *

BEFORE LIGHTNING STRIKES
FULGURATION
HAS STREAKED THE SKY.

PASCAL QUIGNARD

DOES THE BODY LET LIGHT GO THROUGH MORE OR LESS ?

YES.

JACQUES REBOTIER

ONE IS AS VIRTUOUS
AS ONE'S GLANDS.

GEORGES BERNANOS

A naked body is rid of the imperatives of modesty and fashion. Everyone is naked at birth. Nakedness asserts itself with that shared evidence. Should we hide the evidence?
Clothes are complicated masks. We have lost our body hair and that forces us to invent covers in all materials, including taking animal pelts to finally find again the hair we have lost. We used to kill to cover ourselves and to eat. Today we kill for fun.

* * *

On the island of Le Levant, and in other remote places on the planet, territories exist where nakedness is welcomed.
By focusing nakedness on the part of the body that shelters the sexual organs, we access biological nakedness, that of simple convenience, that of all animals.
* * *

BETWEEN SMALL CREATURES THINGS ARE CLICKING AND THAT CAN CHANGE THE WORLD.

NICOLAS CILSOUL

What is Man, and what difference is there between him and other animals? None, that's certain.

SADE

THE IDEA OF DREAMING IS SIMPLE (...), THE SOUL GETS RID OF BODY LIMITATIONS (...) AND EXPRESSES ITSELF IN A UNIVERSAL TONGUE.

PHILIPPE DESCOLA

THESE WATERS SHOULD BE CALLED 'EARTH WATERS', FOR THEY HAVE BUILT THE LANDSCAPE WE LIVE IN.

JEAN-CHRISTOPHE BAILLY

We know them, they swim across the bottom of the oceans like flashes of light, they are bolts of lightning with scales, they shine as in a mirror and reflect the sun from the water. Gold is a makeshift fancy-dress, it is all about amazing the earthlings by assuring them they have caught the right fish, those which resist investment at the stock exchange... Then we can lift them up high, and even pull them out of the water.
We can also make a bouquet with them.

* * *

Gold is not only the concern of anglers at the watershed. It appears as rain on the shoulders of blind traders, it is mixed in with dead branches in the undergrowth, gathered in bunches to light a fire without the use of matches.
In the garden, we find gold everywhere, it doesn't shine, it appears in the shapes and colours of all the flowers. We don't give it a price, we protect it.

* * *

ZOREY HAD AN INCREDIBLE AMOUNT OF MONEY. MY FATHER AND MY MOTHER USED TO LAUGH ABOUT IT, BECAUSE HE NEVER SEEMED TO KNOW HOW TO SPEND IT.

RICK BASS

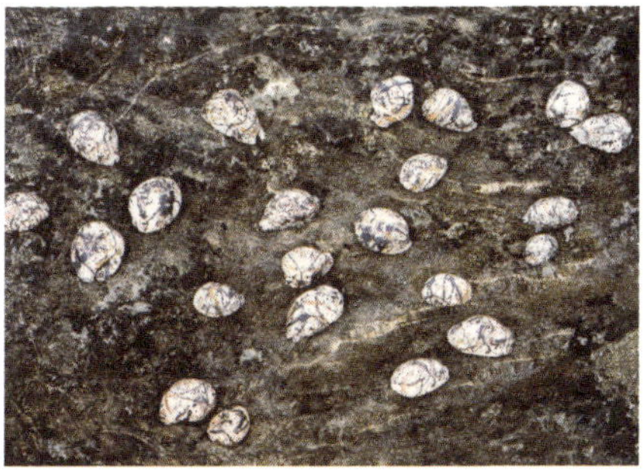

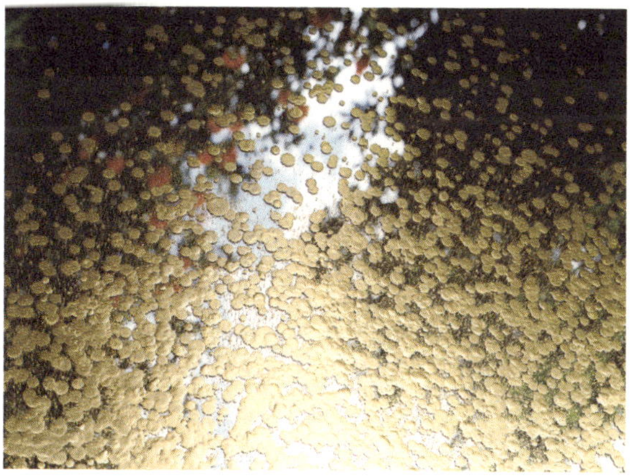

WHAT MAKES LIFE POSSIBLE
IS WHAT WE CAN DRINK,
WHAT WE CAN EAT.
BY CHANGING IT INTO GOLD MIDAS WAS CAUGHT.
YOU CAN'T EAT GOLD!...

MICHEL PIQUEMAL

DON'T YOU SEE THE SEA?
WERE YOU GIVEN LOVE?
TO EACH HIS MOTHER LAND.
IN WAR, HIS HEAVY LOAD.
HOW TO SAIL AWAY?

CYRIL MOKAIESH.

We travel across oceans with or without oars, on foot or floating. Travelling is a suspension whose power we don't measure, it carries us along and makes us understand the place where we live when we return. It surprises us when we come back home with sea urchins on our shoes. That is visible. People can point their fingers at us and denounce us for the illegal shipping of protected species.

* * *

No problem with what is not visible: tiny seeds stuck to the bottom of trousers, bacterial dust infiltrated in tissues. Everything travels. As it always did.
The maple tree seed is equipped with a wing that spins in the air like the blade of a helicopter. The least breeze carries it away. .

* * *

THE WIND THAT HOWLS OVER THE SEA (...) LIKE VIOLINS OVER THE ATLANTIC THAT SING THE FANTASTIC.

LÉO FERRÉ

BADOIT

IF YOU LOOK AT THEM RIGHT, IF YOU REALLY LOOK AT THEM,

ALL LIVING CREATURES ARE WORTHY OF FABLES.

BAPTISTE MORIZOT

LOOKING AROUND THE LANDSCAPE, HE EXCLAIMED 'POPOI'. WHICH IN HOMER'S LANGUAGE MEANS 'GREAT GODS' BECAUSE THE SEA SHIMMERING IN THE MIDDAY SUN IS TRULY BEAUTIFUL.

JEAN-MARIE CHEVRIER

ONE LEARNS A LOT OF THINGS IN A GARDEN. AND A LOT OF THINGS TOO AT SEA.

TO DECIPHER THE ODYSSEY FOR EXAMPLE, IN ANOTHER WAY THAN ON THE BENCHES OF A SMALL-TOWN SCHOOL.

JACQUES LACARIERE

THIERRY FONTAINE
CHAQUE HOMME
EST UNE ÎLE
nrf

Australia and Amazonia and other forests are burning all over the world. Electric bulbs and metal chains don't care about fire, they pretend to light up and release their flames in the air like we let our hair flutter in the wind. Fire belongs to them, they manipulate it, telling us, with a voice that translates into images: 'Do what you can, we do what we want, especially if it's impossible!'.

* * *

And it burns, it illuminates, it heats the air, it destroys barriers, it makes electric fibres vibrate as they die laughing.
A nail in the mirror doesn't care about shards.
A spider in its web torn by a careless rake remakes the world in less than a day. The gardener knows it and doesn't worry.

* * *

GENERALISED STATE OF ALIENATION THAT SUPPORTS DEMOCRACY LIKE THE LEGLESS CARRY THE BLIND INTO A FOREST ON FIRE.

ERIC CHAUVIER

WHAT DOES THE PAINTING REPRESENT?

THAT DEPENDS ON WHO LOOKS AT IT.

WHISTLER

NATURE DOESN'T HEAL EVERYTHING, ESPECIALLY WHEN THE DISASTER WAS CAUSED BY MEN.

RYOKO SEKIGUCHI

All night long
they drank, among
the huts of the Jacques,
and the flame, longer,
richer, that makes
the roof-frame of
the bourgeois.

Pierre Michon

...TO GIVE EACH PERSON NOT
THE EQUALITY OF OPPORTUNITIES.
**THAT TALL TALE
INVENTED TO REINFORCE
COMPETITION
BETWEEN INDIVIDUALS**
BUT THE POSSIBILITY OF CHOICE.

CORINNE MOREL DARLEUX

The *travelling soul* produces dreams with vigour. The sedentary soul is timid: it cannot construct a game by comparing distant elements suddenly brought together. Sometimes even bound together. Bringing them closer give birth to hybrids, mixed-races and ecosystems emerging all over the planet. Whether in nature or in culture.
The mechanisms of evolution function that way: the living receives a message, makes it complex and sends it back.

* * *

With an Eiffel Tower made out of shells or a coconut transformed into a football, we receive a message from Europe or America coming from Vanuatu or Swaziland.
In the garden, Mexican orange blossom mixes with Japanese andromeda, and all is well.

* * *

WHAT IS THE IMAGE WITHIN THE IMAGE?

THAT IS WHAT IS THERE, BUT THAT I CANNOT SEE.

WHAT THE EDITING REVEALS
THAT WOULD REMAIN HIDDEN WITHOUT IT.

GILLES TIBERGHIEN

SOMETIMES YOU ACCUSE ME OF NOT BEING UP TO DATE AND YOU DON'T REALISE I'M ALREADY NEXT MONTH.

SACHA GUITRY

SQUANDERING ONE'S TIME IS THE ONE LUXURY WHICH NO ONE THINKS OF TREATING ONESELF TO.

PAUL MORAND

THIS STREET IS AN ASSEMBLAGE
OF LITTLE BITS OF STREETS.

DON'T EVEN THINK
OF TRYING TO FIND
IT ON A MAP.
IT DOESN'T EXIST.
IF IT DID, I WOULDN'T HAVE
SPENT MY TIME MAKING IT UP.

FELLAG

EACH WORD
IS A TREE ON THE FIELD
OF THE PAGE.

A BOOK
IS A FOREST
OF WORDS.
A POEM, A WOOD
OR A GROVE.

JULES VIPALDO

THE ARRANGEMENT OF IDEAS
IS DONE WITH THAT OF OBJECTS.

JULIA V.

Termites make towers out of earth. The skyline of animal cities is in harmony with the horizon of mountains. Human animals indulge themselves in a different way, they build hard walls, cubes, dwellings with right angles. Except for those who look for sensual harmony with the ground.

* * *

For soft modelling, one needs mud, clay, pliable earth that accepts to be manipulated or *footipulated*. One can use fingers or toes, like all of earth's primates.
And so the palm of the hands joins the sole of the feet in a tactile concert. The result is a construction decided by the material itself. .

* * *

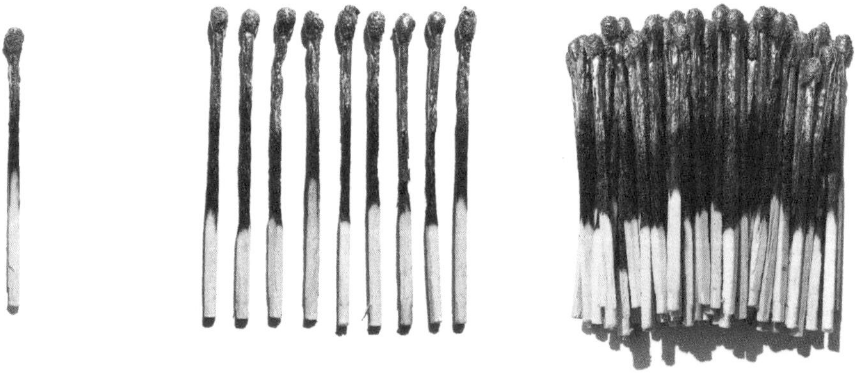

ALL BUILDERS,
IN THE END,
ONLY BUILD A COLLAPSE.

MARGUERITE YOURCENAR

BEAUTY
ESCAPES GOVERNMENTAL
HANDS (...),
IT REAPPEARS IN THE NON-ARTISTS, THE PRISONERS, COUNTRY FOLK AND CHILDREN.
A LITTLE BIT MORE
THAN A CULTURE:
A MASTERLESS
COMMUNICATION.

ANDRE GLUCKSMANN

WE WOULD LIKE THE QUALITY OF AN ARCHITECTURE
TO DEPEND NOT ON ITS EXCESSIVE PROPORTIONS NOR ON ITS SPECTACULAR OR SPECULATIVE ASPECT
BUT ON THE ROLE IT PLAYS, ETHICALLY, IN THE LANDSCAPE AND LIVES WHICH INCORPORATE IT.

EMMANUEL HOCQUARD

BOTANY IS THE ART OF PLANTS. PLANTS ARE DIVIDED INTO TREES, FLOWERS AND VEGETABLES. THE GOOD BOTANIST SINGLES OUT THE TREE AS SOON AS HE SEES ONE. HE LEARNS TO DISTINGUISH IT FROM VEGETABLES BY LISTENING TO IT.

LEACOCK

NOMADS WALK SLOWLY.
THERE ISN'T A SINGLE HORIZON THAT HASN'T CAPITULATED FACED WITH THEIR TENACITY.

SYLVAIN TESSON

To communicate with another person is to risk an emotion. We can't prevent it.
To avoid the wrong encounter, the signal in the prelude must motivate the person who sings as well as the person who listens.

* * *

Not everyone knows that 'Each man is an island', some think the opposite. However, the word 'Alone' is enough to evoke billions of solitudes: clusters of islands, human archipelago. Any language can convey this message. It will be received with the same force from one end to the other of our big shared garden: the planet.
Sometimes, we have to shout in a shell to say it, scream into a microphone or whisper in an attentive ear.
As soon as it is received, it becomes the bond that unites.
Tho gardener works alone for everyone, and everyone knows it.

* * *

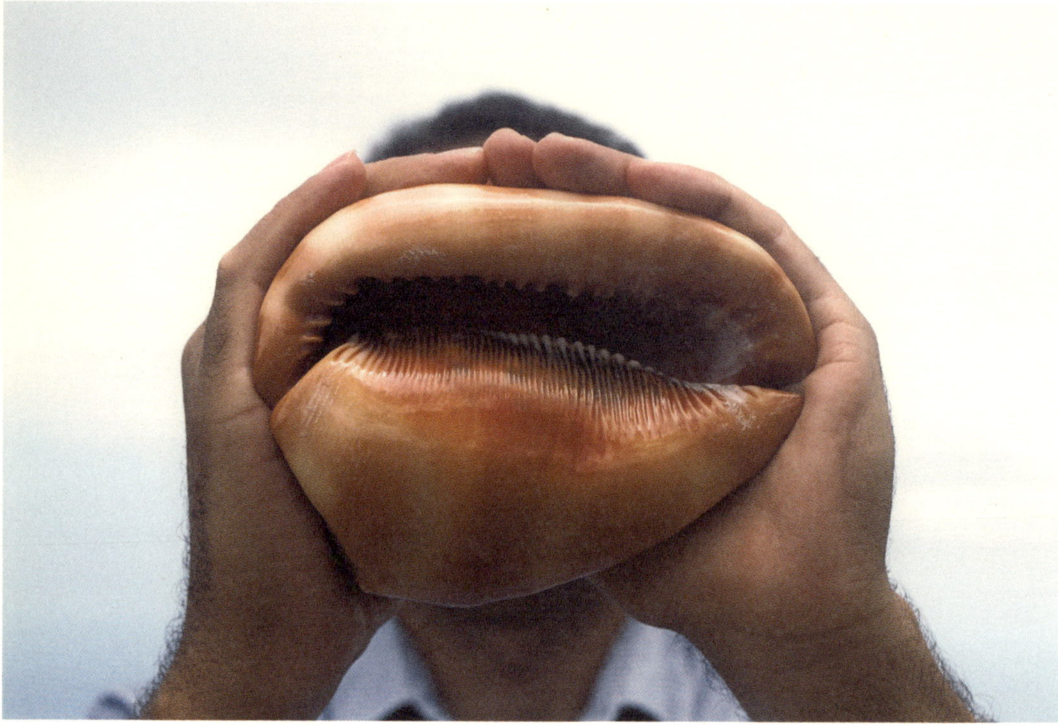

THE ECHO IS THE VOICE,
THE FAITHFUL VOICE, INCLUDING
BENEATH THE VAULT OF SOUND
THAT MAN HAS BUILT.

JEAN-CHRISTOPHE BAILLY

HAVE YOU EVER SEEN A NOMAD IN A HURRY?

SYLVAIN TESSON

SEUL

BIOGRAPHIES

Gilles Clément

is a celebrated French botanist, horticultural engineer, landscape architect and writer. Above all he is a gardener who travels the planet and pursues theoretical and practical work from three research axes, the Moving Garden, the Planetary Garden and the Third Landscape.

Since the early 1970s he has been designing and creating gardens for private clients in France and abroad. In 1977, he stopped this activity to devote himself to public spaces and founded the Atelier Acanthe in 1985. He set up independently as an artist in 2000 and organizes his services in co-contracting with landscape studios, in particular Coloco in Paris.

Several prizes have been awarded to his work, including the "Grand prix du paysage" in 1998. The Parc André Citroën (in co-design), the Domaine du Rayol in the Var, the Arche Gardens in Nanterre, the Jardin de Valloires in the Somme, the Matisse Park in Lille, the garden of the Quai Branly Museum in Paris, and the roof of the submarine base in Saint Nazaire (Jardin du Tiers-paysage) are among the most well-known projects with the public. Teaching at the Ecole Nationale Supérieure de Versailles from 1980 to 2012, in 2011/12 he was teaching at the Collège de France as part of the chair of artistic creation and continues to teach on a temporary basis in the form of workshops in Italy, Spain and France.

He is the author of about thirty books including:

- Environ (ne) ment: Approaches for Tomorrow (Skira, 2006)
- Leendert Blok: Silent Beauties (Hatje Cantz, 2015)
- The Planetary Garden "and Other Writings (Penn Studies in Landscape Architecture) (University of Pennsylvania Press; 2015)
- A Big Garden (Prestel Junior, 2018).

Thierry Fontaine

is a photographer from the Reunion Island, whose images, often poetic, arise from scenes and situations where hybridizations, crossbreeds are imposed or fortuitous. A singular work constructed through a plurality of resources drawn from heterogeneous spheres that are at once artistic, cultural, political and poetic.
His work has been shown in many places,:

Solo Exhibitions

- Centre Photographique d'Île de France -octobre 2018
- FRAC Provence Alpes Côte d'Azur, Marseille, France 2017
- Archipels (dans le cadre du mois de la photo), La Terrasse, Nanterre 2017
- FRAC Provence Alpes Côte d'Azur, Marseille, France 2016
- Le Banian, FRAC Réunion, France 2016
- La Terrasse, Centre d'Art, Nanterre, France 2016
- Les Joueurs, Carte blanche PMU, Centre Pompidou, Paris, 2015
- La part de l'autre, Maison des Arts, Grand Quevilly, France, 2014
- La part de l'autre, Galerie Les filles du calvaire, Paris, France, 2013
- L'envers de l'île, École supérieure d'art de La Réunion, Le Port, La Réunion, 2013
- Journées photographiques de Bienne, Bienne, Suisse, 2013
- Ici la couleur est évidente, Galerie Louise Michel, Poitiers, 2012
- Abbaye Sainte Croix de Poitiers, Abbaye Fontaine-le-Comte, France, 2012
- Changement de Main, Micro-Onde, Centre d'Art Contemporain, Vélizy, France, 2011
- Every Man is an Island, Raw Space Gallery, Brisbane, Australie, 2007
- Chaque homme est une île, Artothèque départementale, Saint-Denis (La Réunion), 2005
- Project Room, Galerie Yvon Lambert, Paris, France, 2003
- Fa, Projects Gallery, Londres, Angleterre, 2001
- Les Sauvages, Musée Léon Dierx, Saint-Denis (La Réunion), 2000
- Fonds régional d'art contemporain, Saint-Paul (La Réunion), 1997

Il a aussi participé à des expositions collectives - entre autres au StudioMuseum, Harlem, New-York, USA, 2008 et en, 2009, au Museum of the African Diaspora, San Franscico, 2016.

Publications[

- « L'invention d'une île, » Thierry Fontaine, Christine Ollier, Simon Njami, Loco Éditions, Paris, 2014
- « Les joueurs » - carte blanche PMU #5, Thierry Fontaine, Clément Chéroux, Gilles Clément, éditions Filigranes, Paris, 2015

INDEX PHOTOS

Masked identities

Eyes dull yet bright

Naked

Gold fish

Arrivals

The impossibles

Cross-fertilisation

Constructions

Messages

SOURCES OF QUOTATIONS

Chapter 1: Masked identities (p.6)

- 'Don't believe that freeing oneself is to be oneself, it is to invent oneself as another self.' - Alain Damasio, 'Le Dehors de toute chose', ed. La Volte, 2016

- 'Faith reveals to us that God created man out of mud and our eyes show us he remains that way.'- R.P. Stockius

- 'Considered from a zoological point of view, in the anatomic properties of his body, Man risks remaining unnoticed, unrecognised, drowned amidst beings that surround him.'- Jean Piveteau, 'Annales de Paléontologie', ed. Masson

- 'The body needs to forget itself in order to think.'- Pascal Quignard, 'Mourir de penser', ed. Grasset

- 'The charm of Je-ne-sais-quoi activated.'- Vladimir Jankélévitch, 'Le Je-ne-sais-quoi et le Presque-Rien', ed. Points

Chapter 2 : Eyes dull yet bright (p.18)

- - 'Reality has more imagination than us.'- Edgar Morin cited by Hubert Reeves in 'Je chemine avec…' ed. Seuil, 2019

- '…they only come in an invisible way, and they reside in masks on days of dancing and celebration in a mystical way…'- O. Mannoni, 'Clefs pour l'imaginaire', ed. Seuil

- 'In love as in beauty, every true look is an exchanged look.' François Cheng, 'Cinq méditations sur la beauté', ed. Albin Michel

- 'Before lightning strikes, fulguration has streaked the sky.' - Pascal Quignard, 'Une journée de bonheur', ed. Arléa

Chapter 3 : Naked (p.28)

- 'Between small creatures, things are clicking, and that can change the world.'Nicolas Gilsoul, 'Bêtes de ville', ed. Fayard 2020

- 'One is as virtuous as one's glands.' - Georges Bernanos

- 'Does the body let light go through, more or less? Yes!'- Jacques Rebotier, 'Description de l'Omme', ed. Verticales

- 'What is Man, and what difference is there between him and other animals? None, that's certain.'- Sade, 'Français, encore un effort si vous voulez être républicains', ed. Mille et Une Nuits

Chapter 4 : Gold fish (p.38)

- 'These waters should be called 'earth waters', for they have built the landscape we live in.'- Jean-Christophe Bailly, 'Couler de source', ed. Bayard, 2018

- '…what makes life possible is what we can drink, what we can eat. By changing it into gold, Midas was caught. You can't eat gold!…- Michel Piquemal, 'Récits fabuleux de la Mythologie', ed. Albin Michel

- 'Zorey had an incredible amount of money. My father and my mother used to laugh about it, because he never seemed to know how to spend it.'- Rick Bass, 'Dans les monts Loyauté', ed. 10/18 domaine étranger

- 'The idea of dreaming is simple (…), the soul gets rid of body limitations (…) and expresses itself in a universal tongue.'- Philippe Descola, 'Reporterre,' february 2020

Chapter 5 : Arrivals (p.50)

- 'Don't you see the sea? Were you given love? To each his mother Land. In war, his heavy load. How to sail away?'- Cyril Mokaiesh. 'Song from the album 'Paris-Beyrouth', 2020

- 'The wind that howls over the sea (…) like violins over the Atlantic that sing the Fantastic.'- Léo Ferré, extract from the song 'Le vent'

-"If you look at them right, if you really look at them, all the living creatures are worthy of fables." Baptiste Morizot in Bayard's "Traquer les créatures fabuleuses".

-"Looking around the landscape, he exclaimed "Popoi". Which in Homer's language means "great gods" because the sea shimmering in the midday sun is truly beautiful.» - Jean-Marie-Chevrier in "La Compagnie d'Ulysse" by Albin Michel

- 'One learns a lot of things in one's garden. And a lot of things too at sea. To decipher the Odyssey, for example, in another way than on the benches of a small-town school.'- Jacques Lacarière, 'Un jardin pour mémoire', Nil éditions

Chapter 6 : The Impossibles (p.62) -

- '...generalised state of alienation that supports democracy like the legless carry the blind into a forest on fire.'- Éric Chauvier, 'Les mots sans les choses', ed. Allia, 2018.

- 'What does the painting represent? That depends on who looks at it.'- Whistler

- "Nature doesn't heal everything, especially when the disaster was caused by men" - Ryoko Sekiguchi in Nagori at P.O.L.

- "All night long they drank, among the huts of the Jacques, and the flame, longer, richer, that makes the roof-frame of the bourgeois..." - Pierre Michon in "Mythologies d'hiver at Verdier's.

Chapter 7 : Cross-fertilisation (p.74)

- '...to give each person not the equality of opportunities, that tall tale invented to reinforce competition between individuals, but the possibility of choice.'- Corinne Morel Darleux, 'Plutôt coulor on beauté que flotter sans grâce', ed. Libertalia, 2019

- 'What is the image within the image? That is what is there, but that I cannot see, what the editing reveals that would remain hidden without it.'- Gilles Tiberghien, 'Notes sur la Nature', ed. du Félin 2005

- 'Sometimes you accuse me of not being up to date and you don't realise I'm already next month.'- Sacha Guitry

- 'Squandering one's time is the one luxury which no one thinks of treating oneself to.' - Paul Morand, 'Éloge du repos', ed. Seuil

- 'This street is an assemblage of little bits of streets. Don't even think of trying to find it on a map. It doesn't exist. If it did, I wouldn't have spent my time making it up.'- Fellag, 'Rue des petites daurades', ed. J.C. Latès

Chapter 8 : Constructions (p.86)

- 'Each word is a tree on the field of the page. A book is a forest of words. A poem, a wood or a grove.'- Jules Vipaldo, 'Pour qui sonne le Douglas?', ed. Les Banquets du Château, 2018

- 'All builders, in the end, only build a collapse.'- Marguerite Yourcenar

- 'We would like the quality of an architecture to depend not on its excessive proportions nor on its spectacular or speculative aspect but on the role it plays, ethically, in the landscape and lives which incorporate it.'- Emmanuel Hocquard, La Bibliothèque de Tanger

- 'Beauty escapes governmental hands (...), it reappears in the non-artists, the prisoners, country folk and children. A little bit more than a culture: a masterless communication.'- A. Glucksmann, 'La cuisinière et le mangeur d'hommes'

- 'Botany is the art of plants. Plants are divided into trees, flowers and vegetables. The good botanist singles out the tree as soon as he sees one. He learns to distinguish it from vegetables by listening to it.'- Leacock, 'Histoires humoristiques', ed. Livre de Poche

- 'The arrangement of ideas ... is done with that of objects.'- Julia V. '... de l'eau suffit', ed. Edivre, 2018

Chapter 9 : Messages (p.100)

- 'Nomads walk slowly. There isn't a single horizon that hasn't capitulated faced with their tenacity.'- Sylvain Tesson, 'Petit traité de l'immensité du monde', ed. Pocket, 2008

- '...the echo is the voice, the faithful voice, including beneath the vault of sound that man has built.'- Jean-Christophe Bailly, 'Le propre du language', ed. Seuil

www.disvoir.com
www.facebook.com/groups/disvoir/

ISBN:978-2-914563-97-0

printed in EUROPE